GLORY GIRL

Also by Jess Connolly

You Are the Girl for the Job

*Take It Too Far: Abundant Life,
Boundless Love, Unending Grace*

GLORY GIRL

DARING TO
BELIEVE IN YOUR
PASSIONS AND
GOD'S PURPOSE

JESS CONNOLLY

ZONDERKIDZ

Glory Girl
Copyright © 2020 by Jessica Ashleigh Connolly

Requests for information should be addressed to:
Zonderkidz, *3900 Sparks Dr. SE, Grand Rapids, Michigan 49546*

Library of Congress Cataloging-in-Publication Data

Names: Connolly, Jess, author.
Title: Glory girl : daring to believe in your passion and God's purpose /
     Jess Connolly.
Description: Grand Rapids, Michigan : Zonderkidz, 2021. | Audience:
     Ages 8-12 | Summary: "Glory Girl, with Jess Connolly's wisdom
     and guided journaling opportunities, will help girls ages 8-12 feel
     confident in who they are as they discover who they are meant to be
     through God"— Provided by publisher.
Identifiers: LCCN 2020023734 (print) | LCCN 2020023735 (ebook) | ISBN
     9780310770152 (hardcover) | ISBN 9780310770169 (ebook)
Subjects: LCSH: Girls—Religious life—Juvenile literature. | Identity
     (Psychology)—Religious aspects—Christianity—Juvenile literature.
Classification: LCC BV4551.3 .C66 2021 (print) | LCC BV4551.3 (ebook) |
     DDC 248.8/2—dc23
LC record available at https://lccn.loc.gov/2020023734
LC ebook record available at https://lccn.loc.gov/2020023735

Published in association with literary agent Jenni Burke of D.C. Jacobson &
Associates, LLC, an Author Management Company, "www.dcjacobson.com."

Zonderkidz is a trademark of Zondervan.

Zondervan titles may be purchased in bulk for educational, business,
fundraising, or sales promotional use. For information, please email
SpecialMarkets@Zondervan.com.

Cover Design: Brand Navigation
Interior Design: Denise Froehlich

Printed in China

20 21 22 23 24   LEO   10 9 8 7 6 5 4 3 2 1

To the original Glory Girl. Gloriana Eloise Connolly—you are a God dream.

Contents

The Day I Didn't Get Picked for Gymnastics Club

Are you in a club? Or on a team? Do you have a hobby that you're awesome at or a musical instrument you're working on learning to play?

I'm going to be honest with you glory girls, from the outset. When I was your age I wasn't really in any clubs or groups. It's not because I didn't want to be—it's just that I wasn't all that great at anything.

I'll never forget the warm November day in fifth grade when I stood in the sunlight outside of school, watching all the gals who were involved in gymnastics. They were flipping around the monkey bars on the playground like they were going for gold at the Olympics. If I wasn't jealous of how cool their moves were, I *definitely* was jealous of their friendships. They'd started a "Gymnastics Club" during recess and you were only allowed in if you knew how to do a move called a "penny drop."

I remember watching them and feeling so behind, so left out, and also so . . . *less than*. Less than what I could be, less than others, less than loved.

This isn't a book about gymnastics and it's honestly not even a book about us, which is good news! My prayer is that you'll find that every single page of this book is about a God who made us good, set us free, and has invited us on an adventure. He is always good enough, and He is always loving us.

This is a book about a God who made you His **glory girl**—a girl who shows the world how great He is and shares His love with others.

This book won't tell you that you've "got what it takes" and help you fit in, but it will point to the One who does have everything and loves you completely. This book won't suddenly make you feel like your whole world is great, but it will encourage you with this truth:

You've been placed where you're at,
on purpose, for the good of those
around you and to spread His glory.

We're going to go on a journey, one that I pray will take you to a place of being able to boldly, humbly say that YOU are His glory girl. More than that, I hope these words help you feel like a leader—a girl who can speak life-giving words to others and remind them God loves them too!

We're going to learn to be others-focused, setting our intentions on their good, which will actually help us fight those less-than feelings that come up. We're going to do some journaling and question answering to help us see how God has made us—specifically what gifts and strengths He's given us so we can serve and love everyone else.

We're going to talk about what it looks like to hear from God! Did you know He wants to communicate and talk with you? We're going to ask Him about what He is doing in our lives and what He wants us to do. Scripture says that if we ask for wisdom, God will provide it. **So we're going to take Him up on that promise!**

This is an invitation to kick off the feels of fear, the lies that tell us we don't belong, so we can get on with the adventure God has for us. It's time for us glory girls to step into the light so God can shine on us and in our hearts, so we can move forward with what He's asked us to do.

And we're not just going to agree with our *minds* that we are His glory girls, we're going to agree with our *lives!*

This is your invitation. This is our invitation. For the girls who feel like they fit in and those that don't. This is for those of us who are sure God has given us strengths and skills and for us girls who don't yet know what those could be. This is for the girls who are scared and those who feel brave but could still use some encouragement every once in awhile. This is for the girls on the fence about God. I pray you'll see His purpose for your life and find your passion for your life.

Let's not miss it! Let's not miss out on the adventure God has for us! Because getting to be in the club (gymnastics or otherwise) shouldn't be the most fun we have. In the family of God, we can fit in, in crazy different ways. We can be used by Him right now, right where we're at, and it will be the most thrilling thing we'll ever experience.

You are a glory girl. You are GLORY, girl. You are a picture of God, a reflection of Him, placed here on earth to serve and love and help others see Him. **You shine and you don't have to hide.**

Are you ready for that?

THOUGHTS OF GLORY

How would you describe your life to someone who's never met you?

....
....
....
....
....
....
....
....

On a scale of 1 to 10, how much do you believe this sentence: God has placed me where I'm at on purpose. Explain your rating.

....
....
....
....
....
....
....
....

What do you think it means to reflect God's glory?

....
....
....
....
....
....
....
....

Do you wish you had more adventure in your life? Why or why not?

....
....
....
....
....
....
....

Quit Before You Start

The day I was left out of the gymnastics club, I wish I had done something different. I wish I would have told the girls, "It's SO cool that you're good at gymnastics!" and meant it. I wish I would have encouraged them, because I now know that what I'm great at is encouraging people. But I didn't. Instead, I started a running club.

You might be wondering, "Oh! Were you good at running?!" No! In fact, I was such a slow runner that to be mean my t-ball team called me "lightning." I wasn't a good runner, but I wasn't good at gymnastics either. I just wanted a THING.

I wanted a thing to be known for, to be measured by, to be grouped with. I wanted something to be *really* good at.

Do you have a thing? Something that's all yours? That people know you for? Have you ever wanted one?

You may not care a thing about gymnastics and

running might not be on your radar. But those are easy examples for us to think about. It doesn't change the truth that somewhere in your life there is probably a temptation to fit in somewhere or to stand out.

Where in your life is the desire to look at other girls and compare yourself to them? Maybe you'd never admit you're trying to be the best but I am sure it's there.

Maybe you thought that being a glory girl is all about being great or awesome and knowing it! Maybe you wondered if you qualify to be a glory girl at all because you've never been awesome at anything. The great news is that no matter whether you feel special and seen or forgotten and last place, the first step is the same for all of us. **We need to quit before we start.**

Being a glory girl is about giving God glory. And we can't seek God's glory and our own at the same time. Let's unpack this a little. What is glory? Who should get it?

Our Father in Heaven, He's the best. He's the King and He's here for His glory. Because He has called us His girls and given us work to do, we have a race to run. But it's not a race we're trying to beat others at. It's not a race in which we win the prize and claim the glory for ourselves. It's *His* race, aimed at bringing as many other people into His family as possible.

Dictionary.com defines glory as something that is a source of honor, fame, or admiration. The Bible agrees with that definition in that God is full of glory.

He is glorious! God is amazing—amazingly good, amazingly kind, amazingly personal. And He's made us to be attracted to glory. When we see something beautiful, we can't look away. We want to be near things, people, and situations that are incredible or awe-inspiring. But our lives can get very tripped up when we start to crave glory for ourselves. Essentially, that's us wanting other humans to worship us. That would be pretty silly and crazy, right? I mean, I wanted those girls in the gymnastics club to like me, but I didn't want them to start singing songs to me and wearing sweatshirts with my name on them. That would have been silly.

But still, there was something small and yucky in my heart that day. I wanted their attention. I didn't want God to have their attention. I also wanted their approval! And in wanting these girls to see me and like me, I missed the very crazy news that *I already had God's attention!* What did I need theirs for?

The Most Glorious One—the God who made the oceans and the stars and humans and giraffes and the Grand Canyon—He already sees me and pays attention to me because He loves me.

I could have quit trying to be seen, trying to be the best, trying to gain approval right there because I already had God.

So here's the bad news. It's really hard to be a girl giving God glory—a glory girl—if we're trying to be

3

the best and have everyone tell us how great we are all the time. We miss out on so much of the adventure and the amazing things He has in store for us if we're busy trying to get our own glory.

So, see? We NEED to quit it before we even start!

Keep your eyes on *Jesus*, who both began and fin-ished this race we're in. Study how he did it. Because he never lost sight of where he was headed—that exhilarating finish in and with God—he could put up with anything along the way: Cross, shame, what-ever. And now he's *there*, in the place of honor, right alongside God.

HEBREWS 12:2 (MSG)

We're going to spend the rest of the book working to understand what it means to be a girl who is out for God's glory. But I want you to know up front THE REALLY GREAT NEWS about quitting before you start:

You are off the hook.

It's God's grace, God's strength, God's power, and God's gifts in your life that get so much of the work done. You don't have to worry about getting the glory for yourself, and you also don't have to worry about try-ing to become someone great. You already *are* great because God made you purposefully and powerfully in His image.

THOUGHTS OF GLORY

You are off the hook from needing to do something phenomenal or becoming something amazing or incredible yourself. God already is. How does that make you feel?

....
....
....
....
....
....
....
....

How have you seen God's grace, strength, and power in your life so far?

....
....
....
....
....
....
....

To really understand what it means to be a glory girl, we're going to quit before we get started and become excited about God getting the glory instead of us. And there's a lot of freedom in this for those of us who are convinced we'll never be enough and are not actively trying to be the best either. So we're going to look at a Bible story about a well-known character who gave God much glory but initially thought he couldn't.

In the Old Testament, we find a group of people who were God's people—His chosen ones, the Israelites. Their story starts much earlier than we will here—we're just looking at one part of their history. And we're going to eventually get to another famous guy, Moses. But first let's start with **Joseph**.

Joseph was one of Jacob's sons—in fact his favorite. His brothers were so jealous of this relationship. They plotted and sold him into slavery. Joseph could have been bitter and hateful but God was planning. So even after the awful things his brothers did to him, Joseph was a man willing to be used by God, excited to use his gifts of wisdom and vision to serve others. In Genesis 25, Joseph saves his brothers (after they'd done those awful things to him) right as the whole country was about to experience extreme famine, or lack of food and water.

God had already warned Joseph about this famine through a dream when he was younger and given him wisdom on how to take care of everyone—and included in that "everyone" were his mean brothers, who he forgave and offered to help! Joseph was living in Egypt and after he rescued his brothers, they moved to Egypt as well.

Joseph did *not* miss his moment to be used by God. He could have been selfish and denied help to his brothers, but he didn't. And his obedience to God led to them all staying alive and well. They didn't *just* stay alive and well, however. Their family grew and grew until they weren't just one family that the Egyptians allowed to live in their land. They became a growing people group that eventually made the government leaders nervous. Joseph was long dead and he wasn't there to assure the new leaders. Many years after the Israelites first arrived in Egypt a new pharaoh, or king of Egypt, was in charge and became so threatened by these Israelites, he made them slaves.

But the Israelites were strong and this hardship only made them grow closer to God and stronger yet, which of course made the Egyptians even *more* fearful of them. And this led to Pharaoh declaring that all the Israelite baby boys must be killed (to stop the Israelite group from getting bigger and stronger).

This is one of the parts of the Bible that is hard for me to read, because it's so sad. I'm a mom and I love people and I get sick to my stomach hearing that one person would be so obsessed with his own power that he would order babies to be killed at birth. But that is exactly what Pharaoh commanded. And as we look at Moses's life and the events that were happening in Egypt, it's important that we know this part of history *really* happened.

Hard things happen in this world now and they've been happening throughout time. You, glory girl, are probably just beginning to hear and see some hard things—maybe on the news or at school. Hard and horrible things happen to good people, but this is what I love about God: He's always there with a rescue plan.

Some people ask, "Where is God?!" when hard things happen, but we see in the book of Exodus that God was THERE, using *people* to be the helpers, the rescue plan. God was so sad over the pain His people were experiencing so He worked out a plan to help them. Our Father is not hiding in times of injustice. Instead He is often preparing and using His favorite rescue plan: *people.*

Where is God in the midst of pain? He's working miracles we couldn't dream of. He is asking normal people, like you and me, to meet the needs and fight for the good of others. God is not hiding—He is just working out a plan that allows us to be part of the rescue.

And this next part of the story of the Israelites, the story of Moses, is what we find in the book of Exodus.

God is asking normal people, like you and me, to meet the needs and fight for the good of others.

Moses was born in the middle of this extreme pain, in the season when Pharaoh was forcing midwives to kill Israelite babies at birth or to throw them into the Nile River. Specifically, they were killing all the *male* babies, since in their culture nobody thought girls were all that powerful or special anyway. As we walk a little further into Moses's story, there's something important I want us to see that will make this story mean even more to us.

Certain cultures may not think girls are very important—but God does. In fact, He invited many girls to help and be His coworkers in the fight against injustice in this story. Pharaoh ordered that all the little baby boys be killed, but he made the big mistake of forgetting the power of God in the girls that would rise up and fight on God's team. Midwives (those who helped birth the babies) like Shiphrah and Puah fought by disobeying his law, Moses's mother would fight by hiding her son, Moses's sister Miriam would fight by organizing his rescue, and God would even use Pharaoh's daughter to save Moses, the baby who would grow to be the man who helps God's people finally escape from Egypt.

Big mistake, Pharaoh. You can forget how powerful girls are, but God never does!

Let's make no mistake that God can work through crazy supernatural things, He can work through the wind and the waves. But He chooses people like you and me to work with Him as He fights the pain in this world. Make no mistake that He wants to use you, YOU, to fight the darkness that lives around you. Make no mistake that we're still in the middle of God rescuing the world, that He is still in the process of setting things right. Let's not make the mistake of missing it because our eyes are focused on ourselves, or because they're overwhelmed by the size of the fight, or because we're waiting for a hero to do the work for us.

Although he had plenty of moments of obedience and faith—Moses almost missed it. Don't *you* miss it!

What do you say to God?

Now we're going to run through more of Moses's story. His mother hides him, his sister, Miriam, works the plan to save him, the daughter of Pharaoh raises him as an Egyptian prince, but God pricks Moses's heart for *his true people,* the Israelites. As a young man, he sees an Israelite being beaten, murders the Egyptian who beats the Israelite, and then out of fear and shame flees to a place called Midian. Moses stays in Midian, where he marries a woman named Zipporah and is seemingly happy, pretending as if his people aren't still in a lot of pain back in Egypt.

Who doesn't forget? **God**. And He goes to Moses with an offer.

Let's read part of it together:

Moses was shepherding the flock of Jethro, his father-in-law, the priest of Midian. He led the flock to the west end of the wilderness and came to the mountain of God, Horeb. The angel of God appeared to him in flames of fire blazing out of the middle of a bush. He looked. The bush was blazing away but it didn't burn up.

Moses said, "What's going on here? I can't believe this! Amazing! Why doesn't the bush burn up?"

God saw that he had stopped to look. God called to him from out of the bush, "Moses! Moses!"

He said, "Yes? I'm right here!"

God said, "Don't come any closer. Remove your sandals from your feet. You're standing on holy ground."

Then he said, "I am the God of your father: The God of Abraham, the God of Isaac, the God of Jacob."

Moses hid his face, afraid to look at God.

EXODUS 3 (MSG)

If you've never heard that story, it's a little crazy and amazing, right? A burning bush? God talking out loud to a human? It's wild stuff! Let's thank God right now that sometimes He gets really loud and active to get our attention. But let's keep going with Moses's story. God is about to invite Moses into something really big. Way bigger than gymnastics club.

God said, "I've taken a good, long look at the affliction of my people in Egypt. I've heard their cries for
deliverance from their slave masters; I know all about
their pain. And now I have come down to help them,
pry them loose from the grip of Egypt, get them out
of that country and bring them to a good land with
wide-open spaces, a land lush with milk and honey,
the land of the Canaanite, the Hittite, the Amorite,
the Perizzite, the Hivite, and the Jebusite.

"The Israelite cry for help has come to me, and
I've seen for myself how cruelly they're being treated
by the Egyptians. It's time for you to go back: I'm
sending you to Pharaoh to bring my people, the
People of Israel, out of Egypt."

EXODUS 3: 7–10 (MSG)

I want you to put yourself in Moses's shoes for just
a moment now. God comes to you and tells you He
REALLY CARES about this huge problem in the world.
He's going to solve it but He needs your help.

THOUGHTS OF GLORY

What do you think your response might be?
How do you think you might answer Him?
Journal about that here before we go any
further in Moses's story.

....
....
....
....
....
....
....
....
....
....

Thanks for being honest as you answered. Let's see what Moses said:

Moses answered God, "But why me? What makes you think that I could ever go to Pharaoh and lead the children of Israel out of Egypt?"

"I'll be with you," God said. "And this will be the proof that I am the one who sent you: When you have brought my people out of Egypt, you will worship God right here at this very mountain."

Then Moses said to God, "Suppose I go to the People of Israel and I tell them, 'The God of your fathers sent me to you'; and they ask me, 'What is his name?' What do I tell them?"

God said to Moses, "I-AM-WHO-I-AM. Tell the People of Israel, 'I-AM sent me to you.'"

God continued with Moses: "This is what you're to say to the Israelites: 'God, the God of your fathers, the God of Abraham, the God of Isaac, and the God of Jacob sent me to you.' This has always been my name, and this is how I always will be known."

EXODUS 3: 11–15 (MSG)

I want you to imagine what your friend, your parents, grandparents, or teacher would say to you if you were scared to do something.

They might say, "Don't be worried! It's going to be great!"

They might say, "You've got what it takes!"

They might say, "Everyone gets nervous! You've practiced, just do your best!"

You'll notice God doesn't say any of that to Moses because God has something else *He* can say that no human can. God doesn't promise Moses that Moses can do it. He promises that *He* (God) has what it takes.

THOUGHTS OF GLORY

When Moses asks, "Why me?" how does God respond?

....
....
....
....
....
....
....

Let's read the last little bit of Exodus 3 together.

"Now be on your way. Gather the leaders of Israel. Tell them, 'God, the God of your fathers, the God of Abraham, Isaac, and Jacob, appeared to me, saying, "I've looked into what's being done to you in Egypt, and I've determined to get you out of the affliction of Egypt and take you to the land of the Canaanite, the Hittite, the Amorite, the Perizzite, the Hivite, and the Jebusite, a land brimming over with milk and honey.'

"Believe me, they will listen to you. Then you and the leaders of Israel will go to the king of Egypt and say to him: 'God, the God of the Hebrews, has met with us. Let us take a three-day journey into the wilderness where we will worship God—our God.'

"I know that the king of Egypt won't let you go unless forced to, so I'll intervene and hit Egypt where it hurts—oh, my miracles will send them reeling!—after which they'll be glad to send you off. I'll see to it that this people get a hearty send-off by the Egyptians—when you leave, you won't leave empty-handed! Each woman will ask her neighbor and any guests in her house for objects of silver and gold, for jewelry and extra clothes; you'll put them on your sons and daughters. Oh, you'll clean the Egyptians out!"

If the questions we're left with after hearing that we are glory girls are: *why me?* and *how will I bring God glory?* the story of Moses tells us that we're asking the wrong questions.

The answer to "Why me?" is this: *God is who He says He is.* "How could you use me?" **He'll** *be the one doing the hard work.*

God doesn't tell Moses all the reasons why Moses has got this, He just tells Him: I am. I am your Father. I am the one who has helped you and will help you again. I am the hero. *I am who I said I was and you can trust that!*

I can boldly declare that you are a glory girl, without knowing you or your life, because I know God. Because

I know He's all powerful, all knowing, always loving. I know that He wouldn't leave you behind or fail to give you what you need. Because He is the starter of our faith and the finisher, and the story writer of every human on earth. I know that He's working it all out for us to experience the most of Him that we can—for us to see and show His glory.

The thing is, *I just don't want you to miss it. I don't want us to miss it.*

God is not going to stop showing up or walk away from us. He's not going to give up on His plan of using girls to bring Him glory—no matter how unready we feel.

We've got work to do, glory girls! Our world is hurting, our friends need Jesus. God has placed you in this exact slice of time—arranging every relationship, circumstance, strength, weakness, and gift in your life to prepare you to shine His light and build His kingdom.

But we have to settle something here and now, before we start looking at the tools He's placed in our hands.

We have to quit telling God (and ourselves) that we don't have what it takes. We also have to quit wanting to fit in or stand out or be the best. Remember, that's about *our* glory and we were meant to bring **Him** glory. And in the name of Jesus, we've got to quit telling God He's got the wrong girl.

- God is God. God is the Hero. We are blessed to be a part of His rescue plan.
- God is God, but we are the girls He has chosen to bring light and life to where we are, to who we are with.
- If we believe He is in control, then we can trust what He says about us: *we are His glory girls— placed here to find our passion and fulfill His purpose.*

Let no one say otherwise. Not even us!

THOUGHTS OF GLORY

There is a moment in a glory girl's life when she acknowledges that she needs God and wants to live for His glory. Have you experienced that moment?

....

....

....

....

....

....

What would it look like for you to keep your eyes on Jesus in your everyday life?

....

....

....

....

....

....

How can you quit trying to fit in or stand out TODAY?

....

....

....

....

Give Him Glory

USE THIS SPACE TO TALK TO GOD about what you need to quit in order to really shine for His glory. Don't forget you can ask Him for wisdom and then listen for His answers.

You can't do this wrong—just write what's coming to your heart and mind.

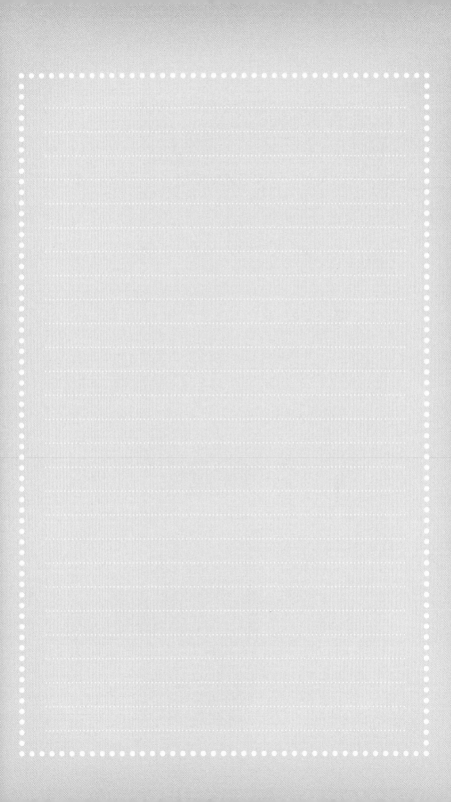

CHAPTER 2

Who Are Your People?

My First F and My Friend Sarah

In fifth grade I knew I was going to be a writer, but it wasn't because my grades were so good. Actually, I got my first F in fifth grade. That's pretty horrible, right? It was extra horrible because my teachers knew that I loved reading and writing. I just didn't try hard enough. Now I wish I had.

What's even crazier: I got my first F in fifth grade, *in English*. But that same year I won a writing award that gave me the confidence to know I had a gift for stringing my words together in a certain way and helping people see something in a new light with those words. I'll never forget my teacher being proud of me for winning the award, while also being frustrated with me for not trying harder in her class.

She was right! But the good news is I was now aware I loved *writing*, not just getting awards for doing it. Words were a ticket to sharing my feelings. Stories were a passage to other places. And I started using them more often.

I would go on to write more in middle school and high school, but I still struggled with my grades a lot. Mostly because I didn't quite understand that I was a glory girl—I was scared to try hard and maybe mess up. If I could go back, I'd try harder in school . . . not to stand out or fit in, but just to make the most of those days of learning!

By the time I got to college I was positive I'd be a writer, but maybe not for the reasons you'd guess. Really it was because of my friend Sarah. My freshman year, God was showing me the passion that He'd given me to feel and the gifts He'd given me to use. I went to college super excited to meet new friends, to learn, and to visit different Christian ministries. I'd heard there were a lot of great ones at the school and I couldn't wait to try them all!

FCA. BCM. SNA. (A lot of them had funny abbreviations!) Worship Nights. Local churches' college ministries. My sister had gone to this same school just three years ahead of me and found tons of Christian friends to connect with, places to serve and lead, and a handful of Jesus-centered events to pick from every single week. This is exactly what I wanted for myself!

The day I moved into the freshman dorms, as my parents hauled boxes up and down the seven floors in the sticky South Carolina heat, I excitedly ran from room to room trying to figure out the answers to the burning questions I had at the forefront of my mind: Which of these gals were Christians and which would be my new friends?!

I squealed inwardly as I noted one gal writing a Bible verse on the tiny mirror that hung in all our dorm rooms. *"Oh, I see you like the Bible! Me too! I love this verse! Do you want to go to church while you're here? I hear there's a big church offering free lunch for college students tomorrow. Do you want to go with me?"*

The next morning, I was up early. I'd convinced eight women from my floor to go to church with me, even though my car only fit a total of five. We smushed in like sardines and drove to church. It was all happening . . . my dreams were coming true!

We had a great morning, but a few weeks later the newness had begun to wear off. Classes had begun and people were getting busy, so my group of new friends was growing smaller—but also larger. There were still one or two girls on my floor that were interested in the same things as me, but I was meeting other people, on different floors and in different buildings, who'd come to college looking for the same Christian friends I was.

But I couldn't move on so quickly. My heart was attached to these gals I'd met that first week and grown to love, particularly to the one with the scripture written on her mirror, the one who'd gone to church with me once and never come back. *Let's call her Sarah.*

Her eyes looked weary, and all the sparkle and sweetness was drained from her face. I could tell she was struggling in those first few weeks of college, trying to find her place. She was looking in the wrong places and it was hurting her, leaving her exhausted and unhappy. One night, I sat with her when she was sick and while I sat there, I prayed, asking God for some way to help and encourage her. I was talking to God, asking Him why He'd placed me on this floor. Why had He let me see her writing that Bible verse on the mirror on move-in day? How could I help?

The next day, I made a decision. In all the praying and listening to God about why I was on that hall of freshman girls, why He'd made me to care so much about their passion and purposes, I'd come up with a plan. I was choosing to believe He'd placed me there on purpose—for our collective good and His glory. I was choosing to believe He wanted me to love them and tell them about Jesus with everything I had. I resolved to show up with my actions, serving them when I could through words as well as actions.

Friday afternoon I took a sheet of paper and a pen, marched down the hall to each of their rooms, knocked on each door, and asked the gals to write down their email addresses. Had I ever written a devotional at this point? No. Did I have any formal Bible teaching? No way. Did I probably say some absolutely crazy things in my devotions? You better believe it. But throughout that year, I just wrote little daily Bible messages—glimpses of grace, hope, love, and abundance. And I sent them to the emails of the ladies who lived on the 7th floor of my freshman dorm, whether they liked it or not.

Did anyone ask me or invite me to do this? Only God. Was I the world's best writer? Not really. Did all the girls love the emails so much and thank me each time they received one? Nope.

But it was a start, and I was burdened for these gals who seemed to be struggling with the same things I was currently struggling with or had struggled with in the past. It helped me process my concern for them, my concern for Sarah. Writing each devotion gave me a safe place to show them that I cared. It was a start that was all about love and wanting to use what I had in me for God's glory.

What I'm saying is this, glory girl:

The starting line to finding your people is often looking for those you can serve, not those who will accept you.

THOUGHTS OF GLORY

In the past, have there been groups of people you've longed to fit in with?

....
....
....
....
....
....
....
....
....

How did it make you feel to be included or excluded?

....
....
....
....
....
....
....

Are there people in your life you already know
God has given you to serve?

....
....
....
....
....
....
....
....

You're Here for Abundance

I see so much confusion amongst girls I meet about
their purpose in life and where they should start. For
me, I was never certified to be a coach and I certainly
didn't feel qualified to tell people what they should
do or how they should do it. But I noticed that as God
grew my influence through writing books and teaching
the Bible, women wanted to know how I got started
and they wanted a little guidance on what **they** should
do next.

I've always thought that I shouldn't call it coaching
because it's more like being a mirror for people. Often,
the best thing I can do for a girl I'm meeting with is
to hold her own passion and purpose back up to her. I

ask her to describe why she wants coaching, where she wants to go, what she is trying to build or grow, and then for the better part of the session I ask a lot more questions! What do you mean by that? What would happen if that fear did come true? Why do you care what they think? Who told you it was going to go that way?

Each girl has the answers, she just needs someone to ask the questions. I think the same is true for you! I think God has given you a purpose and passion, you just need to wake up, get up, and give it room to run.

I think about what might have caused you to pick up this book or what caused someone to suggest you read it. Are you struggling with fear or comparison? Are you feeling excited and pumped up about the future? Maybe you just need a big reminder that you were made to show God's glory to the world.

Do you know what *abundance* means?

Here's what the dictionary says:

Abundance: an overflowing fullness, an extremely plentiful or oversufficient supply.

In the Gospel of John, Jesus says this: *I came that they may have life and have it abundantly.*

I believe you were meant to abundantly experience every single day you're given, waking up with the passion and purpose of God. I believe you were called to change the world, helping more people see how good and glorious He is. I believe your days will be most joyful, your heart will be most free, and your mind will be most at peace when you've said yes to Him! And I believe it will feel worth it when you see other people knowing Him more because He's used you in such a mighty way.

I don't think you were meant to be here on earth and *not* make a difference! I think God has handcrafted you and sent you to use what you've got to forever make a mark on how eternity is played out even in the midst of normal days, tough seasons, and moments when life gets really tough.

I know you're a glory girl, but the story of your life is not meant to be about your glory alone. And honestly, that's a great thing! That means that our dreams and goals get to help others in amazing ways. If the beginnings of our dreams are rooted in us being the hero, how great we are, our desire to be known, or anything that has to do with how awesome *we* are, it just won't be enough. None of those things will give us the strength we need, and we'll be disappointed when it doesn't go how we hoped.

Your dreams and hopes for your life are important— but they're not everything. We, as believers in Jesus, get to do this cool thing where we hear from God and find out what **He** wants for our lives but we have to always remember that in reality, things are often slower and less shiny than we want them to be. If our hope is

The great news is Jesus never asked you to be the *best* to get His love or to be used by Him.

in Jesus and giving Him glory, we win! If our hope is in us living out our dreams exactly the way we picture them, we may be standing on shaky ground and setting ourselves up for disappointment.

We're not only acting in a risky way if we concentrate only on our dreams, we also aren't safe when we build our life on how awesome we are. It's because of this that I'm grateful I didn't really have a shiny story to start with. If I had started building my life on my own accomplishments and talents, I would have been scared of messing up all the time or meeting someone who has more talent than me! And there is ALWAYS someone more talented than me. And you too, probably. Someone you know is a better singer or student or leader. Someone is smarter or kinder. The great news is Jesus never asked you to be the *best* to get His love or to be used by Him. He simply wants US.

When we count on only our own gifts and strengths, we'll be frustrated by the strengths and achievements of others and either never start or quit early when we don't live up to our expectations for ourselves or *other's* expectations of us!

That doesn't mean we toss aside the gifts and talents God has given us! We just don't build our identities and lives around them and how good we can get at them.

Glory Girl! Hold onto those dreams and those gifts, don't throw them off. God has given them to you as a weapon of light against the dark, to fight for His glory. But they're tools you can use; not ground you're going to want to stand on. And let's not be disheartened. The starting line may not be where you thought it was, but it's somewhere so much better.

If we're going to make a lasting impact, if we're going to keep going for the long term, the starting line for our lives has to be God's goodness and HIS strength. The firm ground beneath our feet will be His promises and His purposes for our life. We won't have to fight to find them or look further than where He's placed us. And the room we've been given to run, the path marked out for us, isn't limited by our lack of ability but made endless and aimful by His enduring capacity.

Simply put, if we lean our full weight on God, we'll go as far as He can go, we'll fight as hard as He can fight. We will love as many people as He enables us to love. We will have the energy that God allows us to have. We won't be limited by our humanity but powered by His Spirit. The prize we win at the end will no longer be the celebration of how awesome we are, but the indescribable beauty of His glory on display and the life-giving and life-changing knowledge that we gave all that we had so **He** could get all the praise.

The starting line might not be where you think it is, because we don't get to draw it. And this is good news, because then the pressure's off! It's not about *our* capacity. It has always been about God's, and He has unlimited capacity. So we can stop second-guessing ourselves and lean our full weight on the One who calls us.

THOUGHTS OF GLORY

How does it make you feel to know that you don't have to build your life on your own accomplishments?

....
....
....
....
....
....

Off the top of your head, is there anyone you're excited about serving or loving well in your life?

....
....
....
....
....
....

Murder was Moses's Starting Line

Let's dig back into Moses's story.

When we left Moses, we were really just starting to get acquainted with his life, looking over the broad strokes to begin taking in his life and how God would use his leadership skills to get the Israelites out of slavery and into the land He had promised them.

Let's look back at a big turning point for Moses.

> One day, after Moses had grown up, he went out to where his own people were and watched them at their hard labor. He saw an Egyptian beating a Hebrew, one of his own people. Looking this way and that and seeing no one, he killed the Egyptian and hid him in the sand.
>
> EXODUS 2:11-12 (NIV)

Murder. Those words we just read—let's look at them carefully. Moses had committed an act of rage that couldn't be undone—he took another human's life. Moses was a murderer.

You know what's especially crazy about Moses's story in Exodus? He wrote that book of the Bible. So when it came time to describe all God had done in his life and in the lives of the people of Israel, Moses had to write down this horrible start.

BUT there was one really beautiful thing about Moses's horrible mistake. It was rooted in his love for his people. *He was broken for his people.* So broken that his burden bubbled over into unrighteous rage, but broken nonetheless. He couldn't *not* act on behalf of his people any longer. We obviously shouldn't follow in Moses's footsteps when it comes to getting so angry that we do something we will regret and hurt someone, but we can learn from him in other ways.

What we do not see is Moses sitting in his room in the palace dreaming about how *he* must be destined for something great. What we do not see is him counting his strengths as he watched other leaders, figuring out how he could use what he has to build something beautiful or to unite a nation. If Moses seeming awesome to the world was the goal, he would have done those things. Instead, being faithful to God and serving God's people was his ultimate goal.

We should learn from Moses, not necessarily in his execution, but most definitely in his passion. That brokenness for others is another beautiful starting line we can have for ministry.

So as we look to God's starting line, and lean into God's power and purpose in our lives, ask yourself: What are you broken for? Who are you broken for? And let's also take a good hard look at the brokenness within ourselves to see what God has to work with.

Let's Flip the Script

I LOVE my friends. I love my friends. I love my friends.

But I've had seasons in my life when I didn't have such great friends, seasons when I didn't fit in or I wasn't accepted. And honestly, it was in those seasons that I learned something really important about friendships.

Life can be about finding the perfect group of people who make you feel included or it can be about finding the group of people who help you be who God made you to be.

Some of us have a tightknit group of people we get to hang out with. But no matter how terrific they might be, we still have to ask ourselves the hard questions: Do these friends remind me that I'm a glory girl? Do these friends help me look more like Jesus? Do these friends help me love and serve other people?

Some of us don't have that stellar group and we have to ask another set of hard questions: Do I want friends more than I want God? Do I want to fit in with a group of people so much that I'm willing to change who God made me to be? Am I missing out on spending time with other people because I'm waiting for someone to see me, include me, instead of thinking about who *I* can see, love, and include?

Let's look at Jesus and His friendships. He was literally perfect and could have picked anyone in the whole world to be his crew, but he picked these twelve, seemingly random guys. They were not the shiniest guys or even the truest friends. Peter denied Him, John constantly tried to prove Jesus loved him the most, Judas completely betrayed Him. All of them missed the signs Jesus spent His life giving them regarding what was to come (look up Luke 13:33 or Matthew 16:21) and after He was dead, they went into hiding. Of the twelve who walked with Him and learned from Him, John was present at His death and we know Peter watched from a distance.

Being a glory girl isn't about finding friends that make you the happiest. Instead, it's about walking with the people God has given you even when it's not fun all the time. Being a glory girl is all about loving, serving, and forgiving—and sometimes even needing to be forgiven ourselves.

In this next section, we're going to think about our "friends" in a new way! Maybe in ways you've never thought of before. I pray it will be useful if you have one million best friends or if you feel alone. We all need people who love us and encourage us, but let's also widen our circle and see who else God has put in our path to love.

These Are My People

My daughter, Glory, has a people group she has felt called to minister to almost longer than she's had a relationship with Jesus. When she was as young as four or five, she began waving at homeless people. That sounds sweet and kind and human, but her waving was so extra and precious I can barely describe it.

Let's say there's someone slumped over in a doorway in the middle of a big city with hundreds or even thousands of people passing them every hour. Some people might drop some change in a cup for them, some might hand them a meal they'd purchased, but most would ignore them. And a handful wouldn't even know they were there. Glory will wave until she catches their eye, stooping into their field of vision, and making sure they see her saying hi. She wants people without a home to know she sees them and loves them.

When she was seven, she started enlisting our help to make peanut butter and jelly sandwiches to hand out to the homeless. I buy the supplies and oversee the process as the responsible adult, but for the most part she runs the show. She usually prefers that I sit in the car and watch as she hands meals to her friends. She is not scared—these are her people.

THOUGHTS OF GLORY

Is there a person or a group of people that already come to mind for you when you think about who you could serve or love?

....

....

....

....

....

....

Here's another group of people I want you to think about! Who is paying attention to YOU?

Don't say nobody! Because the truth of the matter is that you see people every single day who are paying attention to you, learning from you, and being changed by you.

Your parents, your siblings, your neighbors, friends at school or in your clubs—every single day you are changing lives with your words and your actions. As long as people can hear your voice, read your sign language, or receive your messages, they're listening to you (even if they . . . or you . . . aren't aware of it). You have been given the power to encourage and speak life to them!

THOUGHTS OF GLORY

Who is already listening to you and how could you encourage them today?

....
....
....
....
....
....
....
....

What if they're older than you?

And don't let anyone put you down because you're young. Teach believers with your life: by word, by demeanor, by love, by faith, by integrity.

1 TIMOTHY 4:12 (MSG)

What if they don't love God?

You are the light of the world. A town built on a hill cannot be hidden. Neither do people light a lamp and put it under a bowl. Instead they put it on its stand,

and it gives light to everyone in the house. In the same way, let your light shine before others, that they may see your good deeds and glorify your Father in heaven.

MATTHEW 5:14–16 (NIV)

What if they already know God? What do I really have to offer them?

Therefore encourage one another and build each other up, just as in fact you are doing.

1 THESSALONIANS 5:11 (NIV)

I could keep going, but the simple fact is this: If you want to change the world, you've got a 100% chance of making an impact if you just love the people around you. It's the ripple effect. It's how Jesus became a household name. One person tells another person what they know to be true and they love each other and it goes on and on.

God determines the starting line for each of us, and He often uses the people we've been given to serve and love to give us direction. Being focused on loving others also helps us fight those feelings of being lonely, left out, or unloved. We're loved by God, rescued by Him, and given purpose and passion to change the world! Let's go show them, glory girl!

Give Him Glory

USE THIS SPACE TO PRAY for YOUR PEOPLE. Who comes to mind when you start to pray? Just ask God for whatever you want for their lives. Thank God for them. Ask Him to help you love them well. Is He telling you anything specific about them? Showing you some amazing ways that He made them that you've never noticed before?

Write your prayers here to God—you can't mess this up!

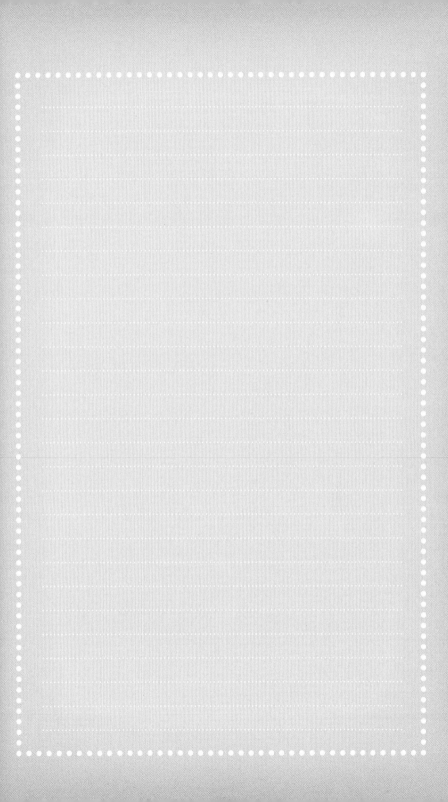

CHAPTER 3

Weaknesses, Strengths, and Purpose

Start with Your Weaknesses

Have you ever done something—said something—so wrong that you immediately wanted to hide?

Literally, this was me yesterday.

Yesterday, I went on a walk with two of my kids and one of them was being pretty awful to me. I was trying to be patient, calm, but suddenly I just lost it. I yelled and said some unkind things. Then I was instantly frustrated with myself. Do you hate when your parents yell at you? I promise *they* probably hate it more when they yell. I love my kids. I do not love when my frustration and sin get the better of me and I hurt them.

Yelling is my *struggle*. And as was demonstrated yesterday, *anger* is my greatest enemy. As soon as it

GLORY GIRL

happened, I turned away, covered my face with my hands, took a deep breath, and turned back.

"Sweetheart, I'm really sorry. I just got so angry and I lost my temper. I said something I really shouldn't have said. You shouldn't have been talking to me that way, but I need to ask you to forgive me."

The thing I love about this kid that I was having the exchange with is that this child is SUPER feisty and stubborn. I know God is going to use that tenacity one day to fight for and change the world, but in this exact moment it was pointed at me and was *not* relenting. So the child actually refused to forgive me and continued to yell back at me for yelling.

But my other child and I kept walking, and here's what was said:

> Elias: Mom, are you OK?
>
> Me: Yeah, bud. I'm so sorry that happened. I'm so sorry I got so angry. Will you forgive me too?
>
> Elias: Of course, Mom. Honestly, I would have gotten angry too.
>
> Me: Well, if you do, please learn from me and pick better words or walk away.
>
> Elias: I actually learned so much from you just now. You stopped and apologized.
>
> Me: *(gently wiping away tears and trying not to cry)*

54

Elias: I think the most important thing we
can know in the world is God. And the
second most important thing we can know
is our weaknesses. And you know this
is your weakness, and you stopped and
apologized. And I learned how to not let
weakness control your day.

Elias is incredibly right. Many of us like to think about what we're good at, but it's really important to know what we're NOT great at as well.

Our weaknesses are real. But we don't have to blame others or hide, because Jesus died for our sins so we could walk in freedom. And more than that, HE KNEW WE'D HAVE WEAKNESSES—and He still placed us where we are to show the world His glory.

But the temptation to hide our weaknesses is there. We see it in the very beginning of God's relationship with man and woman as Adam and Eve are faced with the temptation to ignore God's simple ask of obedience on their life.

When the woman saw that the tree looked like good
eating and realized what she would get out of it—
she'd know everything!—she took and ate the fruit
and then gave some to her husband, and he ate.
Immediately the two of them did "see what's

really going on"—they saw themselves naked! They sewed fig leaves together as makeshift clothes for themselves. When they heard the sound of God strolling in the garden in the evening breeze, the Man and his Wife hid in the trees of the garden, hid from God.

God called to the Man: "Where are you?" He said, "I heard you in the garden and I was afraid because I was naked. And I hid."

God said, "Who told you you were naked? Did you eat from that tree I told you not to eat from?" The Man said, "The Woman you gave me as a companion, she gave me fruit from the tree, and, yes, I ate it."

God said to the Woman, "What is this that you've done?"

"The serpent seduced me," she said, "and I ate."

GENESIS 3:6–13 (MSG)

Both Adam and Eve hide from God when faced with their sin, and both of them choose to blame someone else rather than take responsibility.

It's our nature to blame others for our major weaknesses. But it's our supernatural birthright, bought by the blood of Jesus and made possible by the power of the Holy Spirit, to quit blaming others for our weaknesses and instead allow the grace of God to transform them into something He can use for His glory and our good. We have been given the supernatural ability to let God use our weaknesses so His power can be made perfect in our lives. The days of blame are done. The days of redemption are here.

So how do our weaknesses change the world?

1. We help other people feel more at ease with their own weaknesses when we stop hiding ours.
2. When our weaknesses hurt others and we apologize, everything changes.

Want to change the world? I have three words for you: *say you're sorry.*

If we don't have to hide, we might as well say sorry! Go ahead and repent. Repenting is just a fancy word for saying you're sorry. We can say we're sorry to God, we can say we're sorry to other humans, we can even say we're sorry to ourselves when we're messing up our own day!

This isn't weakness. It is worship. And when we own the things we genuinely could have done better and experience God's grace, it helps other people do the same.

Why spend all this time talking about our weaknesses? Because honestly, I don't think the problem is that most girls don't know what they're good at. I think we're so busy hiding and hiding from our problems, we can't love other people well! So let's quit hiding, acknowledge where we're weak, and let God make us whole.

THOUGHTS OF GLORY

What are some of your biggest sin struggles? Have you told God you are sorry recently?

....

....

....

....

....

....

Are there any weaknesses or temptations you've been trying to hide? What would it look like to confess them and ask for help?

....

....

....

....

....

....

The Best Gift Giver

Do you know your love language? Gary Chapman first wrote about the five love languages in his 1995 book *The Five Love Languages: How to Express Heartfelt Commitment to Your Mate.*

I, for one, am INCREDIBLY grateful for this helpful tool in relationships. The premise is that most people desire to receive love in one or two particular ways and they tend to give love in one or two particular ways. It is important that we know our natural tendencies when it comes to giving love and how we desire to receive it. It's a crazy helpful tool, not just for marriage but for everyone. I'm grateful for the way it has helped me see those that I love and evaluate how they're doing. The different love languages are words of encouragement, physical touch, acts of service, gifts, and quality time.

Three out of my four kids NEED to be touched every day. Even the two older ones who are approaching their tween years and may not ask to cuddle or even initiate a hug. They *need* me to come for them with a cuddle before bed, a pat on the back, or a big squeeze before they get out of the car for school. That's how they receive love, and if I go too many days without giving it to them, I see them get a little ornery. The fourth kid would like to never be touched but craves quality time and gifts like nobody I've ever met.

THOUGHTS OF GLORY

What do you think your love language is? Why?

....

....

....

....

....

....

Check the one you'd rather get:

☐ hug

☐ nice card

☐ surprise present

☐ an afternoon with your friend

☐ someone to clean your room for you

My husband and I have different love languages and that right there is a big old bummer. Let me explain. I tend to give love through words of encouragement and that's also how I like to receive love too. Nick loves through acts of service, which means very little to me. I mean—it doesn't mean nothing! But if I am not watching carefully, I don't realize just how much he's doing to serve me all day long and I won't see how sacrificial and gracious and loving he's being. Likewise, words of encouragement don't mean that much to him. He has a tendency to discount them if he's not careful. He'd much rather have quality time.

If we're not intentional, we can miss each other's displays of affection altogether leaving us both feeling unloved and unseen, when really we're trying to be loving and kind to one another. We have really great days when we both slow down and try to love one another the way we receive it best.

This past summer, as I was writing a book, there were a few mornings in a row when I'd come out of the bedroom at 5:00 am, ready to write, but was honestly dragging from the past day. To my delight, there was a gift on the table from my husband. The Scrabble board, still out from the night before, was arranged in a little love note for me. Simple phrases like, "I love you" or "Keep writing" were arranged with the tiny white letters and as I saw them with my cloudy morning eyes I broke out in the world's biggest smile. I told Nick later in the day how much it meant to me, how encouraged those little gifts left me as I started writing. He paid attention.

Our thirteenth wedding anniversary was a few weeks later and Nick seemed so excited about the gift he had for me. I was blessed to unwrap a Scrabble board with letters glued down, permanently stuck in the arrangement he'd placed them in. All the words

He crafted each
skill you have
with purpose,
with *you* in
mind . . .

filling the board were encouragements, attributes he wanted to affirm over me: *leader, writer, passionate, loving, mother, kind, strong, beautiful.*

The gift was the best ever because it was the one I needed. It was specifically tailored to me, my personality, and emotional needs. I felt seen by him—the giver—loved and known.

I honestly don't deserve a lot of those words. This gift speaks much more to Nick than it does of me. It speaks to his kindness. It tells me who my husband is and reminds me of how he sees me.

If you think about it, the gift always says more about the giver than the receiver. When I told you about this—the intentionality and the thoughtfulness behind the Scrabble board—you probably didn't think: WOW, she must be so impressive to conjure up such a gift.

No, you're just impressed with my husband right now. Just like I was! And that's my point . . . a GREAT gift says far more about the giver than the receiver.

Likewise, God has given you a set of gifts. He had a very specifically designed set of strengths to plant inside you, with full knowledge of how they'd develop and how you would utilize them. He crafted each skill you have with purpose, with *you* in mind . . . not only for your good but for the way you will help others with your intentional set of strengths. He is always thinking about how you can bring Him more glory.

Before we spend even one more moment talking about the gifts God has given you—the strengths our Father has carefully imparted to you—I want to take a moment to remember that when we talk about these gifts, it's the Giver we really get to and NEED TO focus on.

God has not forgotten you and He has not passed over you. *It's time to look with expectation and hopeful eyes, ready to see the strengths our Father has intentionally placed inside you because I know that they're there.*

THOUGHTS OF GLORY

Before we go on a hunt to find your personalized strengths, what do *you* think some of them might be?

....

....

....

....

....

....

....

Name a few important people in your life and jot down what you think some of their strengths might be.

....

....

....

....

....

....

....

....

Tools for the Treasure Hunt

One thing that's really important when we talk about our gifts and strengths is that we can't get stuck comparing what we have with what our friends have. God made our strengths specifically for US! Let's figure out what they could be.

Here are some of my favorite tips and tricks for being on the lookout for the gifts God has given. I invite you to go on a treasure hunt, looking for His goodness expressed to you and through you. We can go with humility and thankfulness—remembering this isn't about figuring out how awesome we are but figuring out how we're made to bring God glory.

Ask A Friend

Hey! Can we talk about something deep? You are my friend. Would you help me figure out the gifts God has given me?

Let's go with the most vulnerable option first since we're such brave glory girls! You only need one honest and gracious friend for this exercise to work but you can always go to two or three if you've got them. You could ask a parent or a sibling too!

I'm on a treasure hunt to find the passion and purpose God has given me. I'm trying to determine my God-given strengths so I can use them for His glory and the good of others. Would you pay attention and tell me what you see in my life?

I'd love to speak into YOUR strengths as well. Thanks, bud.

Ask a friend. Then, give them space to think it over and notice things you never would see yourself. Invite them to join you on this quest to step into God's great and beautiful call on your life.

Use Your Eyes

I believe that our Father gives you eyes to see and ears to hear exactly what you're good at. What is it that you're already doing in your everyday life that is blessing others and changing the world? What comes naturally to you that doesn't to others? You CAN see this.

Are there ways you serve, bless, or love others . . . maybe things that come super easy for you? If we believe that God is the giver of all good gifts, then that means we believe these aren't descriptions of how you're just naturally *better* than others. These are specific gifts He's given you to enact His rescue plan of love where you're at.

What seems to help the people around you? What do you wish more people would help you do? These are God-given gifts that help you give Him glory.

What Do You Love To Do?

I am so thankful God has made it ENJOYABLE for us to use our gifts and strengths! Don't believe that if you love doing something, it must be selfish. If you love writing, write about God for His glory! If you love singing, sing in a way that leads people to worship Him! If you're good with babies, could you serve in your church nursery?

Go Back To Your Weaknesses

Oftentimes when I'm talking to a glory girl who is having a hard time finding her strengths, I ask her what people have criticized her for in the past. I hope you haven't been criticized too much, and I don't want to bring up sad memories, but this exercise can be helpful at times. Sometimes we use what we're great at in the wrong way or at the wrong time, and that's when we're told to stop it.

More than an author or speaker, I'm a communicator. I LOVE TO TALK! I like to communicate ideas, feelings, and emotions, and God made me good at transferring what's in my head to my mouth.

But! I've hurt people's feelings by talking too much, at the wrong time, or sharing an idea or thought too passionately when people aren't ready to hear it. Sometimes it's just the WAY I speak, my tone and volume! I once had a friend tell me that if we were in a serious talk on the phone and one of her kids could hear my voice, they would instinctively start crying.

Am I proud of that? Am I grateful that sometimes the words I say or write hurt other people in the wrong setting or when I use the wrong tone? No. It makes me sad.

But I'm faced with a choice . . . do I bury that gift deep beneath the surface, giving into the fear of using it the wrong way *or* do I keep exposing it to the light, grace, and power of the gospel so I will learn to use my words for good all the time?

If you're looking for strengths, don't look too far beyond your weaknesses. Chances are you'll find some important clues there. Your kindness may look like shyness, or your gift of leadership may look like you're bossy.

But we know better, glory girls! We believe and

affirm that we were made in the image of God, wonderfully and fearfully. We don't stand with our eyes closed and our fingers in our ears, unwilling to admit we can make a mistake. Rather we hold our entire selves—our personalities, our passion, and our purposes—up to God for Him to use how He likes.

Strengths may have been seen as weaknesses, or they may have even been used as weapons in a negative capacity, but they don't have to stay that way.

Give Him Glory

USE THIS SPACE TO TALK TO GOD about your weaknesses and strengths. What they are and what your vision is for how you will use them to give Him glory. Remember—God loves talking to you about YOU and no one knows you better. Ask Him to help you see the things you may not have seen in the past. Thank Him for how He made you.

Just talk to your Father about how He made you!

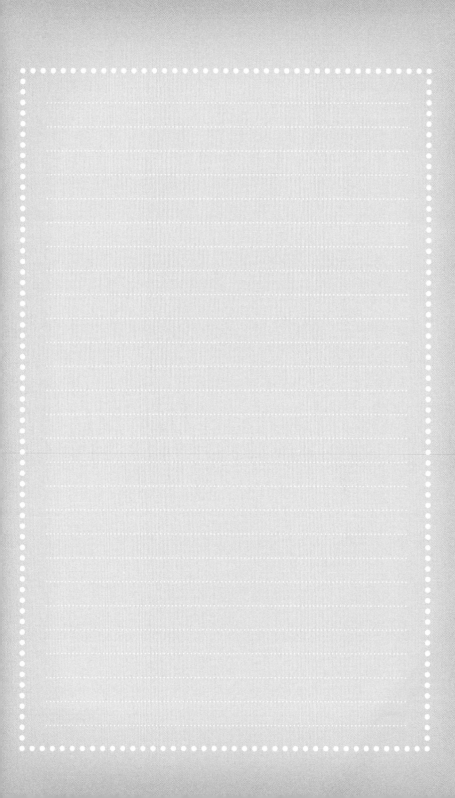

CHAPTER 4

Don't Be Scared

I'll go first.

One night while in college, I showed all my friends just what a scaredy-cat I was. We were on vacation together and my friend Stephanie was with us. Stephanie had a pretty strong fear of elevators, and we knew this about her. I mean we lived in a dorm where she always took the stairs. But this night, for whatever reason, I was kind of bugging her about it. Stephanie and a few girls took the stairs, while the rest of us took the elevator and I started telling the friends who had stayed with me how I couldn't think of anything I was truly scared of. But I was lying, because I'm actually scared of just about everything.

To be funny, Stephanie and the other stairwell gals were waiting at the top of the elevator shaft and they really gently said, "Boo!" when the doors opened. You can imagine the chaos and laughter that came when the gal who was so aggressively declaring she wasn't scared of anything (me!) LOST HER MIND. I screamed, yelled, ran down the hall crying, and banged on our hotel door for someone to let me in . . . because I was SO SCARED.

In general, I am a person that knows fear. I have loved order, structure, and knowing what is next since birth and some of my strongest childhood memories are not joy and wonder, but fear. Not because I had a scary childhood, but because that's the way my brain operated in the past. I let fear rise to the top, giving it the loudest microphone in my life.

So this chapter is on fear and I want to tell you, I'm a glory girl who struggles with fear! If you do too . . . this is for you.

THOUGHTS OF GLORY

What are you scared of? List as many things as you like.

....

....

....

....

....

If you had to pick one thing that you're most scared of, what would it be?

....

....

....

....

....

....

Come Out, Big Alice

A few years back, my older sister became obsessed with the new movie version of *Alice in Wonderland*. She even named her 12-passenger van "Big Alice." I have to admit I giggled at that. But knowing how significant this story became to her, I decided to give it a watch myself. So one afternoon I hit "play" on the remote with my kiddos when they needed some entertaining and the following scene and lines floored me in a big way as we watched the movie.

In this scene from the 2010 version of *Alice in Wonderland*, Alice has shrunk to an incredibly small size and she's so locked up in fear and doubt that she can't possibly see herself as capable of accomplishing what anyone has said she CAN do. What's more, she can't see the danger everyone else will be in if she refuses to act. This is when the Mad Hatter takes Small Alice aside and says:

> *You don't slay.*
> *You're not the same as you were before. You were much more muchier.*
> *You've lost your muchness.*

I sat with my jaw open and heard God say very similar words to me, loud and clear:

You've gotten small to appease other people.

You've let fear and the approval of humans keep you living tiny.

You don't slay, you barely even show up to the battle.

You've lost your muchness.

Since that time, if my sister and I catch each other living in fear or playing it small we bellow over one another, "COME OUT, BIG ALICE!" and we'll remind each other that we're not here for anyone's approval. We were placed on this earth by the King of the Universe to reflect His glory. And that may be too much for some people but it will have to be OK.

You know what else I realized? There was only one difference between Small Alice and Big Alice . . . courage.

Isn't it the same for us? By now, you know where we get our courage: we get courage from believing that God is who He says He is—even who He says He is in us.

The phrase "be strong and courageous" is used roughly ten times in the Old Testament, starting in Deuteronomy 31, when Moses is giving some parting words to the Israelites, informing them that Joshua will be the guy who replaces him. He says not to worry because God will go with them.

> Be strong and courageous. Do not be afraid or terrified because of them, for the Lord your God goes with you; he will never leave you nor forsake you.
>
> DEUTERONOMY 31:6 (NIV)

In Deuteronomy 31 alone, the phrase is used three times. Twice when Moses says it to Joshua and once when God himself says it to Joshua. Be strong and courageous. It's used a total of ten times in the story of Moses and Joshua. Seven of the ten times the phrase is used at the end of Moses's ministry and at the beginning of Joshua's. And then three times in chapter one of the Book of Joshua.

We can look at what the actual Hebrew words mean to understand this verse. Hebrew is the language the Old Testament was written in, and sometimes when verses are translated a lot words can slip from their original meaning or intent. But here, the Hebrew word for strong means . . . strong. No hidden meaning. Courageous in Hebrew means . . . courageous.

Of good courage. Nothing groundbreaking in this phrase. It's just a command from God to be strong and courageous.

Except . . . when God exaggerates His command in Joshua chapter one and changes the language ever so slightly.

"Be strong and very courageous . . ."

JOSHUA 1:7 (NIV)

Why is the word "very" a big deal? And what does this have to do with *Alice in Wonderland?*

"Very" in Hebrew is *meod,* which translates to muchness, force, or abundance.

Be strong and MUCHNESS courageous, God is telling Joshua. Be strong and MUCHNESS courageous, glory girls.

Listening to fear and allowing ourselves to be caged by it can no doubt have incredible consequences in our life. As we see in the story of Moses and Joshua—God gets His plan accomplished, He gets His people free. But it's our opportunity to miss and our blessing to lose when we let fear speak louder than our faith.

When we actually begin to fight fear and face it head on, we will find ourselves slaying—and not just for our own sake. We'll be slaying left and right, and the victory will always be on the Kingdom's side. The

Word of God tells us that perfect love casts out fear, that where there's love there is no room for fear, and that the enemy of our Father and our souls has been defeated and is under our feet.

When we gather the tools we've been given as daughters (princesses even) of the Kingdom, that we need to fight the fear, we are going to experience freedom in ways we could never even ask for or imagine—but we might seem like a little much. We may just have to make a fuss. It may be that we don't seem small anymore, as if we no longer fit in the cages that the enemy would like to keep us in. We also will outgrow the confines that our culture would rather us fit inside.

Sister—my friend—you were made in the image of God . . . not given a spirit of fear or timidity at birth but born into a spiritual heritage of strength and courage that at times will look like muchness to the world. It may seem a little extra. It may ruffle feathers. It may rock the boat. It will absolutely call those around you to evaluate whether or not they're obediently listening to the Father with all that they have. But what is the alternative?

We weren't meant to move forward in our God-given dreams in the midst of fear. We weren't made to be small. He placed us here to slay. For His glory, and our good, and even for the sake of abundant adventure.

That muchness you thought was your liability? It turns out it's your secret weapon. Come out, Big Alice, you weren't made for fear.

THOUGHTS OF GLORY

Write a quick letter encouraging yourself to be strong and courageous.

....
....
....
....
....
....
....
....
....
....

So What Are You Scared of?

I have found that most of us, no matter our age, are scared of three things: not fitting in or not being accepted by others, failure, and being uncomfortable.

THOUGHTS OF GLORY

Which one of those three fears is the biggest fear for you? Why?

....

....

....

....

....

....

....

....

Fear of Rejection

The fear of rejection is the root of the fear of not fitting in or not being accepted. This is one fear that almost all of us struggle with in one way or another.

I believe with all of my heart that if we let the truth of God's Word spread wildly in our hearts, so much will change. So much will be healed. And we'll move into every single day no longer scared about fitting in and ready to stand out.

So let's go with the bad news first:

You WILL be rejected. Yes, you will be rejected.

Let's rephrase that: you most definitely will be rejected. At some time, in some place, you're not going to fit in or you're going to feel left out, someone or some large group of someones will not accept you.

At some point in your life, you are going to come up against rejection. Someone (or many) will take a short glance at you (or a long look) and decide: *I don't like this. It's not for me.*

It may be because you like Jesus too much. It may be because you're too kind. It may be because you're too pretty, or not, in their eyes. Perhaps you are too smart or not smart enough. You might say too much or too little. You might not fit in because you did something wrong or because you refuse to do something wrong.

Why am I being so discouraging? So that the next part will be the most encouraging of news—the best news yet! No matter what rejection you face or how it happens, you're in good company. This is Jesus's story!

Here's a prophecy spoken about Jesus thousands of years before His birth:

> He had no beauty or majesty to attract us to him, nothing in his appearance that we should desire him. He was despised and rejected by mankind, a man of suffering, and familiar with pain. Like one from whom people hide their faces he was despised, and we held him in low esteem. Surely he took up our pain and

bore our suffering, yet we considered him punished by God, stricken by him, and afflicted. But he was pierced for our transgressions, he was crushed for our iniquities; the punishment that brought us peace was on him, and by his wounds we are healed.

ISAIAH 53:2–5 (NIV)

Years and years after that prediction in Isaiah, Jesus would speak about not fitting in:

If the world hates you, keep in mind that it hated me first. If you belonged to the world, it would love you as its own. As it is, you do not belong to the world, but I have chosen you out of the world. That is why the world hates you.

JOHN 15:18–19 (NIV)

At the end of the day, this one—rejection—isn't really worth fearing because it IS going to happen. We ARE going to be rejected. We just get to decide how we're going to act when it happens.

Jesus's response to rejection was compassion, love, and moving on. He never yelled, "OH, YEAH—YOU DON'T LIKE ME?!" at followers who turned away from Him. Rather He had compassion on them.

Here's the definition of compassion: a feeling of deep sympathy and sorrow for another who is stricken by misfortune, accompanied by a strong desire to alleviate the suffering.

So why feel compassion for someone who is being unkind and rejecting YOU? The quick answer is this: someone was probably unkind to them. They may be insecure themselves and that's why they're rejecting you. They may not know God, which is super sad for them. They may have friends who require them to fit in exactly so and now that's what *they* expect.

There are a million different reasons for why someone is unkind, but no matter the reason they all end up with their heart not being a super warm and inviting place. And when someone rejects us, we can feel embarrassed or mad or angry, or we can stop and pray for them.

THOUGHTS OF GLORY

Is there someone who has made you feel like you didn't fit in in the past? Could you stop and pray for them now? What would you pray?

....

....

....

....

So . . . the bad news is that your fear is real—rejection is on the way.

The good news is that once again, Jesus has the comfort and answer you need. *You're in good company! You were NOT put here on earth to win a popularity contest. You're a glory girl. You're here to reflect His glory—not to fit in and reflect someone else.*

The world around you is hurting. But God is the hero and you are a part of the rescue plan! This life is not about making sure that everyone likes us. Let's be glory girls who are prepared to not fit in, who are more concerned with loving others than being loved by everyone else.

Fear of Failure

I find that most of us are scared to mess up, but we're scared of failing in different ways. Here are some of them:

We're scared people will see us fail.
We're scared God will see us fail.
We're scared we'll know we failed.

People + Failure

Have you ever been worried about disappointing your parents, your teachers, or maybe your extended family? This is fear of failure!

Drag the scary truth into the light and ask two questions: "What if?" and "So what?"

What if people see you fail and so what if people *do* see you fail?

What if people see me fail and they are disappointed in me? What if I don't meet their expectations and they no longer think I'm important, good, or worthy of being around? What then? What will happen?

Honestly, they will know you're human. They'll know you're just like them. Then they will have a choice: to pull you closer and take a step toward you because people love the idea of humans being human together *or* they'll push you away and take a step back, because they wanted you to be perfect, which they're not either. I find that people who push you away when you fail do so because it reminds them of their own failures and makes them uncomfortable.

Just like we can have compassion when people reject us, we can have compassion when people are mad at us for failing. Be aware that somewhere along the way, they were told they couldn't mess up—so they don't want us to either.

You're totally going to mess up at some point! It's how you handle the mess up that matters. Can you say sorry, ask for forgiveness, and move on? Even if they're disappointed, you will both grow from that scenario.

THOUGHTS OF GLORY

When was a time someone was disappointed in you for failing in some way? What happened? What did you learn?

....

....

....

....

....

....

God Will See Me Fail

When we were utterly helpless, Christ came at just the right time and died for us sinners.

ROMANS 5:6 (NLT)

How about we don't use *my* words to tell you what happens when God sees you fail and use His instead!

Sin didn't, and doesn't, have a chance in competition with the aggressive forgiveness we call grace. When it's sin versus grace, grace wins hands down. All sin can do is threaten us with death, and that's the end of it. Grace, because God is putting everything together again through the Messiah, invites us into life—a life that goes on and on and on, world without end.

ROMANS 5:20–21 (MSG)

But he said to me, "My grace is sufficient for you, for my power is made perfect in weakness." Therefore I will boast all the more gladly about my weaknesses, so that Christ's power may rest on me.

2 CORINTHIANS 12:9 (NIV)

Let's end with this one:

For we are his workmanship, created in Christ Jesus for good works, which God prepared beforehand, that we should walk in them.

EPHESIANS 2:10 (ESV)

Sometimes I need the gentle reminder that I can't fail with God because He never expected me to be perfect!!! More than that . . . He knows everything before it happens. That means He even knew what I was going to do wrong.

THOUGHTS OF GLORY

How does it make you feel to know that God never expects you to be perfect?

....
....
....
....
....
....
....
....

I Will See Me Fail

Most of you are right around the age when you begin to hear your friends (or yourself!) describe someone as a "perfectionist." I'm giving it to you straight, glory girl, I am no perfectionist. But when I was your age, I was starting to tell which of my friends were.

Perfectionists might be the ones putting all the pressure on themselves to do it right, to get it right, to work as hard as possible. But make no mistake here, the fear of failure is behind that!

As we go through life, we learn to let people off

the hook. We learn to extend the grace that God has extended us. But we have to start with ourselves! We have to be kind with ourselves and not beat ourselves up with the words we say about how we're performing or what we look like. Often, if I hear a friend talking unkindly about herself, I'll say: "Don't talk about my friend that way!"

Do you know who calls you their friend? JESUS!

"I'm no longer calling you servants because servants don't understand what their master is thinking and planning. No, I've named you friends because I've let you in on everything I've heard from the Father."

JOHN 15:11–15 (MSG)

When you're being hard on yourself, I want you to picture Jesus himself saying, "Hey! Don't talk to my friend that way!" He never expects perfection from you! If you make a mistake, try again. Admit when you're wrong, but don't get overly sad or frustrated with yourself. You've got another shot.

Fear of Being Uncomfortable

I don't like being uncomfortable one bit. I don't like being too sweaty or wearing something too itchy. I don't like getting a sunburn that irritates me or having to sit too long in the car. I bet you don't *love* those things either.

But there is a different kind of discomfort that really changes the way we live and reflect God's glory and it's worth paying attention to. That's when we're uncomfortable because we're trying something new or scary, out of our comfort zone and in a beautiful way for God.

THOUGHTS OF GLORY

Have you ever done something that you felt God wanted you to do and it made you feel uncomfortable? What happened?

....

....

....

....

....

....

....

The Bible says that we WILL lose our comfort if we live in a way that brings Him glory. But this is a great time to shake our heads and ask: Isn't that really what we wanted anyhow? Did we want to get to the end and say, "Well at least I was comfortable?"

I feel like we know enough about one another at this point to know that the answer is . . . NO! Glory girls, we are made in the image of Christ. We want what He wants. We want to bring Him glory! We want to change the world! We want more people to know Him. We want to know more about Him ourselves! And we're OK if we get a little uncomfortable in the process, isn't that right?

The bad news is that even if you don't willingly choose it, you'll probably be uncomfortable at some point in the future. You might as well be uncomfortable being obedient to God! Because here's the really good news:

When you're uncomfortable, you can be COM-FORTED by God. And He is better than hot chocolate, a shower, a good book, or even a friend giving you a hug.

> The Lord is my shepherd, I lack nothing.
> He makes me lie down in green pastures,
> he leads me beside quiet waters,
> he refreshes my soul.
> He guides me along the right paths
> for his name's sake.
> Even though I walk
> through the darkest valley,
> I will fear no evil,

for you are with me;

your rod and your staff,

they comfort me.

PSALM 23: 1–4 (NIV)

The world will tell you that if you get good things and surround yourself with the right people, you'll live a happy life. But the world lies sometimes . . . hard things can happen no matter what you do! To good people! Hard things happen to God's people! But we get God and we get to be comforted by Him in the process, and that is amazing news.

What We Know So Far

Some of our fears are very real even though we may never encounter some of them. But we can't let them boss us around *and* believe that Jesus is King at the same time. There is so little we have control over—what will happen to us, what other people will do, what will happen in life. But we do always have the option to love God and love His people.

And perfect love casts out fear.

Let's be glory girls who love, not limited by what *might* come our way. Let's be glory girls who are motivated by our trust in God!

Give Him Glory

USE THIS SPACE TO PRAY about your fears. Remember that God isn't and will never be frustrated with you, rather He wants to help you feel braver. Tell Him what you're scared of and ask for help. He is your biggest fan and He wants you to feel as free as He's made you to be!

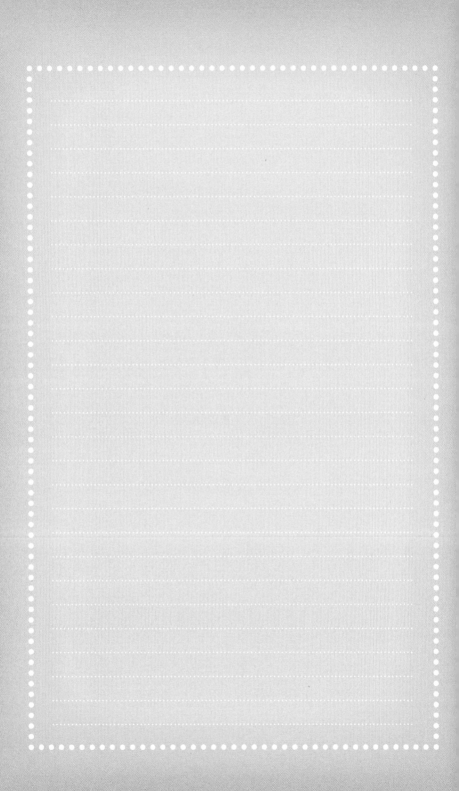

CHAPTER 5

God Talks to You

America's Got Talent

Do you guys like *America's Got Talent*? My kids LOVE IT and recently one of my kids, who is about your age, got an idea.

One day this past summer, said kiddo watched their first episode of *America's Got Talent*. *America's Got Talent*, or AGT for short, is a reality tv show that's also a talent competition, and my kids were hooked QUICK after they watched their first episode. After a few days and a few more episodes, this one child cuddled up to me on the sofa and said they had a serious conversation that needed to be had. I put down what I was doing, faced them, and gave them my full attention.

Anonymous Child: "I would like to try out for *America's Got Talent*."

Me: "Um. OK. For what talent?"

Anonymous Child: (a shocked and offended look on face) "Are you serious? Singing, of course."

Me: "You like to sing? I mean, I've honestly never heard you sing. I'm just a little surprised. You've never been in a choir or even had a singing lesson."

Anonymous Child: "Right. I'm just naturally talented. And I'd like to go on *America's Got Talent*."

Me: (flabbergasted) "OK. OK. Well, um . . . why don't we start with singing lessons and see how you are at singing?"

Anonymous Child: (stone cold serious) "I'll agree to go to singing lessons *once* if you'll listen when they tell you that I don't really need lessons and I'm ready for *America's Got Talent*."

Me: (again, flabbergasted) "I really wish I had your confidence and vision for life."

Weeks of conversation followed, weeks of talking to this incredibly headstrong kid of mine who was absolutely and irrevocably dedicated to the vision they had for singing on stage at *America's Got Talent*. And while there was a huge part of me that was so impressed by this stubbornness, I knew this was the wrong vision to get started.

This kiddo didn't see the practices it would take to become great at singing. They didn't see the necessary learning so they could establish a solid foundation in music. They couldn't think through what determination it would take.

This kiddo also wasn't thinking about anyone else . . . how does the singing serve others or help anyone.

All they could see was the stage. And sometimes, all **we** can see is the stage too. In a lot of ways, we sometimes start with a dream that is all about our own glory, comfort, and joy. And by doing so, we miss out on the very best parts of being girls who reflect *God's* glory.

THOUGHTS OF GLORY

Have you ever had a dream for your life that seemed crazy, but made you super excited? What was it?

....

....

....

....

....

....

Don't Take My Word For It

Did you know that the apostle Paul wrote 28% of the New Testament, with four of those books being written from jail? He was doing incredible work for God, but it probably wasn't his "dream" for his life. One of those books, originally written as letters, was to the church of Philippi—a church Paul had helped start on his second missionary journey. The letter is about a lot of things, but it's particularly about joy and gratefulness.

Can you imagine writing a book about joy and gratefulness from jail? And you are in jail, not for doing something wrong, but for doing what God told you to do?

I think we can learn a lot from Paul when it comes to having a vision for our lives. It's good to dream with God. It's good to want Him to use you in mighty and awesome ways (like He used Paul, even from prison)! But we can sometimes get sidetracked when our dreams only include us on the stage getting all the attention. Sometimes the most amazing ways God can use us include writing to other people, because we really love them, even when it's not a really happy time for us. His dream was encouraging other people to follow God. It didn't matter if he wasn't living "the dream" while He did it! This can be the same for us.

Paul's dream was encouraging other people to follow God. It didn't matter if he wasn't living "the dream" while He did it!

Rejoice in the Lord always. I will say it again: Rejoice! Let your gentleness be evident to all. The Lord is near. Do not be anxious about anything, but in every situation, by prayer and petition, with thanksgiving, present your requests to God. And the peace of God, which transcends all understanding, will guard your hearts and your minds in Christ Jesus.

PHILIPPIANS 4:4–7 (NIV)

Try It, You'll Like It

Here's the thing, glory girl . . . I mean it when I say you get to dream WITH God. I believe that if you trust Jesus as your Savior, you get to HEAR FROM GOD. I believe that He will give you visions and dreams and ideas for your life that are incredible and exciting. I believe that He'll speak to you in cool ways and in crazy places. But I don't want to talk too much about it without just encouraging you to try it for yourself. Before we dig into this even more, here are a few questions.

THOUGHTS OF GLORY

Do you feel like you've ever heard from God?

....

....

....

....

....

....

....

....

Have you ever heard anyone else talk about hearing from God?

....

....

....

....

....

....

....

....

Are you scared you might hear wrong?

....

....

....

....

....

....

....

Here are some of my favorite verses about God talking to His people:

Whether you turn to the right or to the left, your ears will hear a voice behind you, saying, "This is the way; walk in it."

ISAIAH 30:21 (NIV)

All this I have spoken while still with you. But the Advocate, the Holy Spirit, whom the Father will send in my name, will teach you all things and will remind you of everything I have said to you. Peace I leave with you; my peace I give you. I do not give to you as the world gives. Do not let your hearts be troubled and do not be afraid.

JOHN 14:25–27 (NIV)

I have much more to say to you, more than you can now bear. But when he, the Spirit of truth, comes, he will guide you into all the truth. He will not speak on his own; he will speak only what he hears, and he will tell you what is yet to come. He will glorify me because it is from me that he will receive what he will make known to you. All that belongs to the Father is mine. That is why I said the Spirit will receive from me what he will make known to you.

JOHN 16:12–15 (NIV)

If any of you lacks wisdom, you should ask God, who gives generously to all without finding fault, and it will be given to you. But when you ask, you must believe and not doubt, because the one who doubts is like a wave of the sea, blown and tossed by the wind. That person should not expect to receive anything from the Lord. Such a person is double-minded and unstable in all they do.

JAMES 1:5–8 (NIV)

Here's the plain way I explain those verses:

Jesus was sent so that we might become friends of God. He paid the price for our sin, and defeated death and sin when He rose from the dead, stepping in to be punished so we could have a relationship with God.

But that relationship doesn't only happen in heaven!

Because of the Holy Spirit, the wild and beautiful nature of God works on earth, even when Jesus isn't physically here. The Holy Spirit is God HERE—in our hearts, in our lives, in our homes, in our words and mind. And Jesus was constantly telling us how it would be *better* for us when the Holy Spirit came. He assured us that the Holy Spirit would give us guidance, wisdom, comfort, peace, and company.

And I believe with all I've got that there is no reason the Holy Spirit would want to hold back with y*ou*. I believe what God's Word says—that if you ask for wisdom, you'll get it. I believe that God gets excited about giving good gifts and one of the best gifts He gives is direction. He tells us where to go to get help giving Him more glory.

> Do I think He always gives the direction in a
>   dream? No.
> Do I think He always tells us every single little
>   step? It hasn't happened that way for me.
> Do I think there's any reason He'd hold back from
>   you? No.

With all that I've got, I believe that as much as you want God, He wants to give you Himself even more.

So are you ready to talk to God about YOUR life? Here are a few things to remember:

1. It's not weird to hear from God—it's in the Bible!

When something doesn't fit in, when something isn't standard, when it's not like everyone else or its surroundings . . . we call it weird. Like when someone sits alone in the cafeteria, it's because the other people have decided they're not quite "normal."

But often, in the way God works, things are "weird" because they're right. Because they're good and holy. They stand out because everyone else isn't necessarily noticing God and what He's up to. In the Bible, and in our lives, looking like a glory girl often will seem weird. But! Don't dismiss things that seem weird! Remember . . . we're not here to fit in! Reflecting God's glory and loving people like God does is ALWAYS better than fitting in.

You were never meant to fit in, glory girl. You can hear from God—that's not weird! It's wonderful.

If you had to choose between feeling weird and hearing from God, which would you choose. Why?

....
....
....
....
....
....
....
....
....
....

2. It's not up to you whether you hear from God or not.

This is great news. It's important that we remember it's not only the smart or special people who hear from God. And it's not the people who work the hardest or even listen the hardest. When God wants to communicate with you, He will.

When God wants to talk with you, He will not wait

until you're perfect or until you're adequate. He knows that date is not on the way. He wants your willingness to hear—that's it.

If you feel like you won't hear from God because you've messed up, just tell Him you're sorry and move forward. Remember that He has always talked with normal people, with messy people, with mess-ups, since day one and He is not shocked by your secrets.

THOUGHTS OF GLORY

Do you know any Bible stories about people who hear from God? Did they "deserve" it or earn it? (Even if you think you don't, remember Moses!)

....
....
....
....
....
....
....
....
....

3. There are a lot of ways to hear from God.

When we ask God to help us dream about what He wants to do in our lives there are a million (maybe a billion!) ways He can talk to us. He may give you dreams. He may put thoughts in your head. He may give you encouragement through another person. He may talk to you through your parents or your friends who love God. He may talk to you through a song or impart perspective through a message you hear from a teacher or pastor.

I don't know how God will talk to you, but I do know He loves talking to you! Nothing is off limits for Him!

THOUGHTS OF GLORY

Are there any creative ways you've heard from God or learned from Him in the past?

....

....

....

....

....

....

....

4. His Word is the test.

I knew a woman who felt like she was supposed to tithe an extra few dollars because she found it in her car. My sister felt called to start a business as she drew on a napkin while on a mission trip. So what happens when God does bring the vision? How do you know it's Him?

My mom once got direction for her life ministry from a dream about a country music artist. I felt stirred to minister to a homeless woman while watching a movie. Nick, my husband, heard God call him to plant a church while on a drive in the car. If I see the same checkout gal at Trader Joe's two or three weeks in a row, I count it as a sign I should probably invite her to church!

These are just a few examples of God speaking to people that were kind of out of the blue. How do I know these things are of God and not just people putting words in God's mouth so they could do what they wanted to do anyhow?

The Word. In all of these scenarios, if I unpacked what and why each of those people thought God was saying what you'd hear is that all of them lined up with the Bible.

For example, the business my sister started after she was drawing on that napkin? It's a fashion company that makes beautiful skirts. But! The skirts are made in Africa and made by women who need jobs that are safe. By selling their clothing, my sister is able to help provide justice to people across the world.

That helps her obey the scripture Micah 6:8: "He has told you, O man, what is good; and what does the LORD require of you but to do justice, and to love kindness, and to walk humbly with your God?"

To do this ourselves means we have to know the Bible . . . or be willing to look around in it when we need answers!

THOUGHTS OF GLORY

How would you look around in the Bible if you were looking for answers? Who could you go to if you needed help checking something?

....

....

....

....

....

....

....

....

The most important thing I want you know in this moment is this:

God doesn't just listen to you—He wants to talk to you! And He wants to talk to you about YOUR life. Get with the real Author of it all and see what He wants to say.

Give Him Glory

USE THIS SPACE TO TALK TO GOD about your dreams—past, present, and future. Remember that He'll never laugh at you or make you feel silly for having hopes or visions of what's to come! Describe in as much detail as you can, any pictures He's given you of your future. God likes us to dream about using His gifts to the fullest.

CHAPTER 6

You're the Author Now

It's Your Turn

I love writing! I love books! I love reading books!

But glory girl, we've got a potential problem if I'm doing all the talking and you're doing all the listening. You don't get a chance to say in your own words what passions and purposes God has been bringing to the light in YOUR life.

You've read a lot of words! You've answered a lot of questions! You've read about Bible characters and a lot about God himself. But now I want to hear about you.

I think saying some real words will move you forward with all the passion and all the purpose He has given you. So here's my big ask—and please don't skip this part! Even if takes weeks or months, will you promise to really answer these questions for me?

THOUGHTS OF GLORY

How did you feel when you started this book?

....
....
....
....
....
....
....

How do you feel now?

....
....
....
....
....
....
....

Before you began this journey, what did you feel like you needed to do to measure up, fit in, or impress people?

....
....
....
....
....
....
....
....
....
....

How do you think God sees you?

....
....
....
....
....
....
....
....
....

What Bible verses encourage you about how
God sees you?

....

....

....

....

....

....

....

....

....

What were you scared of before you read this
book?

....

....

....

....

....

....

....

....

....

What is true about those fears now?

....

....

....

....

....

....

What are you passionate about?

....

....

....

....

....

Who are you passionate about?

....

....

....

....

....

....

What are your strengths and gifts—the ones God has given you to use? Here are some examples: Are you a great leader? Maybe you could volunteer to lead classes of younger girls at church. Do you love serving your family and friends? Do you like to sing? Write? Help your siblings with their schoolwork?

....

....

....

....

....

....

....

....

....

....

....

What are the weaknesses that you need God's help with? Our weaknesses are some-times easier to notice than our strengths. Do you struggle with talking more than you listen? Are you nervous or often scared in new situations? Does your temper get the best of you? We've all got weaknesses—God is eager to help us with them!

....
....
....
....
....
....
....
....
....

How do you hear from God?

....
....
....
....
....
....
....
....
....
....

What have you heard from God lately?

....
....
....
....
....
....
....
....
....
....

Are there any fresh dreams or ideas that He's given you while reading this?

....
....
....
....
....
....
....
....
....
....

What does it mean to you to be a "glory girl?"

....
....
....
....
....
....
....
....
....
....

What will it look like for you to keep moving forward—reflecting His glory and loving those around you? Be specific!

....
....
....
....
....
....
....
....

It was always important to me that we end this journey with YOU as the author. My words can help, but what you say about your life, what you say about you and God, is most important.

As long as God has me on this earth, I'll be trying to use what I've got for His glory and the good of others. But I'm also looking to you now, glory girl! We need your voice. We need your gifts! The world is better with you in it. You make the colors brighter and the family of God more exciting.

You are His glory. You show His glory. You make Him smile.

It's your turn.

Give Him Glory

USE THIS SPACE TO FINALIZE this season with God. What have you learned about Him since starting this book? How have you changed? Thank Him for all that He's done and ask Him for any help you think you're going to need going forward. Because you WILL keep on growing and changing! Glory girls know that their Father is always listening—say anything and everything that you need to!

Acknowledgments

Thank you to Mary Hassinger for lovingly shepherding this book to where it needed to be. Huge thanks to Jenni Burke for championing this glory girl (me) at all times! Thank you to Deb Hopper, for raising three glory girls and giving us room to run. Anna Victorson, you help me dare to believe in my own passion and God's purpose. Nick Connolly—you get credit for eternity for having two wild women share your home. Thank you for being the pastor, father, and friend that we need. Connolly boys, thanks for giving us extra bathroom time and the comfiest seat on the sofa. Thanks for cheering both Glo and I on as we write. Glory, thank you for being you—I can't wait to see how He glistens your entire life in the light of His goodness and grace.

Hey, Glory Girls!

Connect with Jess Connolly!

 facebook.com/jessaconnolly

 @jessaconnolly

 @jessaconnolly